THE SILVER AGE OF

SUPERMAN

THE GREATEST COVERS OF

Action Comics

FROM THE '50s TO THE '70s

ARTABRAS

A Division of Abbeville Publishing Group

NEW YORK • LONDON • PARIS

TEXT: Mark Waid
EDITORS: Amy Handy (Abbeville) and Steven Korté (DC Comics)
DESIGNER: Sandy Burne
PRODUCTION EDITOR: Owen Dugan
PRODUCTION MANAGER: Lou Bilka

Superman created by Jerry Siegel & Joe Shuster.

The covers reproduced in this volume were provided from the private collections of Joe Desris and Mike Tiefenbacher. All cover credits researched and assembled by Mark Waid.

The captions note the pencil and ink artists for each cover as could best be determined; however, as it was not standard practice to credit artists in the comic book industry until the last few decades, this list may not be definitive. While the authors have endeavored to identify all of the artists involved, they apologize to any person misidentified or not identified and invite such person to inform them of the error.

First edition
10 9 8 7 6 5 4 3 2 1

Library of Congress Cataloging-in-Publication Data
The Silver age of Superman : the greatest covers of Action comics from
      the '50s to the '70s / [text, Mark Waid]. — 1st ed.
         p.   cm.
      Includes index.
      ISBN 0-89660-055-6
         1. Superman (Comic strip)   2. Comic book covers—United States.
      I. Waid, Mark.   II. Action comics.
      PN6728.S9S55   1995
      741.5'973—dc20   95-3952

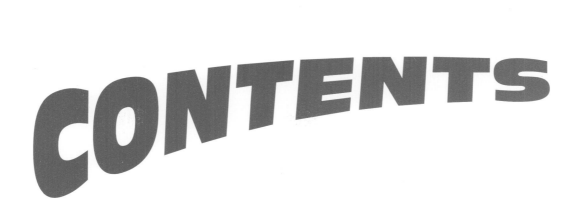

CONTENTS

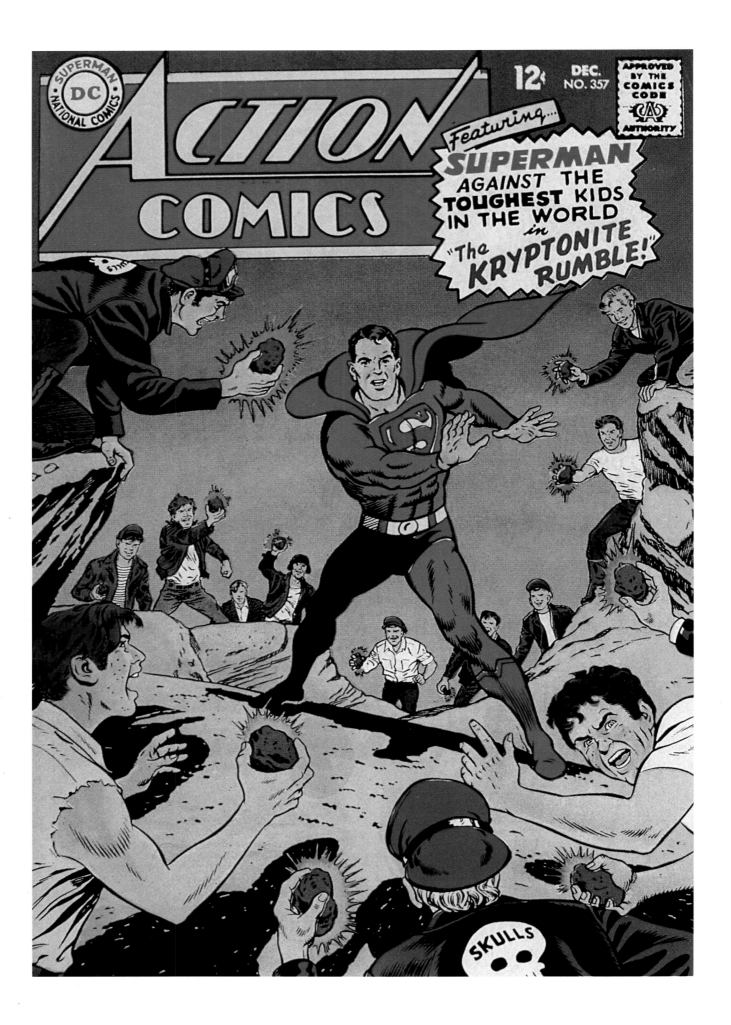

INTRODUCTION BY MARK WAID

Nothing quite like him had ever come before.

In 1938, in the landmark first issue of *Action Comics*, a unique costumed strongman exploded onto the pop culture landscape. Certainly, countless fables of American folklore had been spun around hard-working, hard-fighting men of strength and fortitude . . . but this caped, flying wonder created by writer Jerry Siegel and artist Joe Shuster was something altogether fresh. He wasn't a legend of yesterday. He was the Man of Tomorrow.

His name was Superman.

Though not of this earth, he was still the grandfather to all the countless thousands of comic book heroes who would follow. His instant success sparked a popularity that would blaze a trail—and a presence that would spread like wildfire.

Superman's trademark blue suit and red cape soon became an icon of the era. His presence was felt in every cultural medium. He was novelized in hardcover,

animated and serialized in movie theaters, stripped into the comics section of newspapers, heard in radio adventures, and seen on toys and novelties from board games to bubble gum cards. In short, he was able to leap beyond the label "passing fad" with a single bound.

By the time *Action Comics* entered the Silver Age of Comics in the late 1950s, the Metropolis Marvel's popularity was at its peak, thanks in no small part to the exposure granted him by the outrageously successful syndicated TV show *The Adventures of Superman*. He was featured regularly in the pages of *Superman;* in *Superboy* and *Adventure Comics*, both of which told of Superman's exploits as a teenager; in *Superman's Girl Friend, Lois Lane* and *Superman's Pal, Jimmy Olsen;* and, with others of his ilk, in *Justice League of America* and *World's Finest Comics*. Still, *Action Comics* was his true home, the only monthly publication devoted to chronicling his exploits.

The guiding hands behind all but a

few of the covers reproduced in this volume belonged to editor Mort Weisinger and artist Curt Swan. Weisinger knew that *Action Comics* sales depended on intriguing, thought-provoking, exciting artwork; Swan, the definitive Superman artist of the Silver Age, delivered it with style. Unlike most of today's hypermuscled comics and movie heroes, Swan's Superman was a study in quiet power, a champion equally able and anxious to solve a crisis with brainpower as with super-strength. As such, he was rarely given the chance to change the course of even one mighty river during Swan's tenure; Weisinger preferred cover illustrations that depended as much on surprise and gimmickry as on action—meaning that many of the best-remembered elements of the Superman legend made their first appearance during this era.

For instance, the first Silver Age addition to Superman's fabled gallery of villains debuted in *Action Comics* 242: Brainiac, android super-computer from the planet Colu. As Superman learned, Brainiac's unique modus operandi involved shrinking and bottling entire cities—including Kandor, former capital of Krypton, ripped from that planet's surface mere days before its explosion. Though Superman managed to liberate the miniature metropolis from Brainiac's spaceship, he was unable to restore it to full size.

Fortunately, the Bottle City of Kandor found a new home inside Superman's Fortress of Solitude, the Arctic lair introduced in the previous issue of *Action Comics*. There, the Man of Steel nestled his microscopic kin among the gigantic trophies and intergalactic zoo specimens that comprised the Fortress's treasures. The Kandorians were kept in the safest place on Earth; the contents of the Fortress were sealed behind an impossibly large door that could be unlocked by a massive golden key only its owner could hope to lift.

Superman nearly met his match in *Action Comics* 254, when the chalk-faced Bizarro sprang to life in Frankenstein fashion courtesy of Lex Luthor's imperfect duplicating ray. Though every bit as powerful as Superman, Bizarro's great failing was that his brain was every bit as granitized as his face; simple and childlike, Bizarro's every instinct invariably called for him to do the exact opposite of what a normal man might. In time, the lonely creature populated an entire distant planet with duplicates of himself and Lois Lane (cover 263) and developed a unique credo for its inhabitants: "Us do opposite of all Earthly things! Us hate beauty! Us love ugliness! Is big crime to do anything perfect on Bizarro World!"

During the Silver Age, Superman shared the pages of *Action Comics* with guest stars like Mighty Maid, Mental Man, and Luma Lynai, the Superwoman of a remote orange-sunned galaxy. None of them, however, proved as long-lived as Supergirl, Superman's younger cousin, who fell to Earth in *Action Comics* 252. Despite the cover copy ("Is She Friend or

Foe?"), Superman instantly showed her a love and affection that only a Kryptonian no longer alone could express. Setting her up with her own dual identity—Linda Lee, the newest ward of Midvale Orphanage—he spent many months secretly training her in the use of her powers before presenting her to an embracing world.

Real-life guest stars gave Superman some lighter moments as well. In 1967, Clark Kent met TV's Allen Funt and narrowly escaped having his secret identity exposed on coast-to-coast *Candid Camera* (cover 345). Three years earlier (cover 309), he endured a similar scrape when circumstances required Superman and Clark Kent to appear side by side on national television. In order to preserve the integrity of his dual identity, the Man of Steel raced to find someone who could pose as Clark. Readers were kept in sus-

pense regarding Superman's elegant solution until the story's final panels—when "Clark" revealed himself to be none other than then-president John F. Kennedy. In the words of Superman himself, "I knew I wasn't risking my secret identity with you! After all, if I can't trust the President of the United States, who can I trust?"

Beginning in 1970, at the end of comics' Silver Age, Superman became the sole star of *Action Comics*—and today, a quarter-century later, the comic that gave birth to the super hero remains Superman's home. As he has in the past, the Man of Tomorrow will undoubtedly keep moving with the times as he enters a new age. But no matter how much he may change and evolve, he'll always be the first of his kind. Nothing quite like him had ever come before . . . and nothing quite like him will ever come again.

MARCH 1971; NO. 398
Cover artists: Neal Adams, Dick Giordano

METROPOLIS MARVEL

Faster than a speeding bullet, more powerful than a loco-
motive . . . these well-known phrases barely begin to
describe Superman's vast array of superpowers. His in-
vulnerable body can withstand the impact of the fiercest
blow (covers 200, 231) or the pressure of the deepest sea
(cover 244), while his great strength and speed allow him
to tame wild animals (cover 201) and sink battleships
(cover 214). In fact, not only can he leap tall buildings in
a single bound, he can build them miles high (cover 228)
or crumble them with one punch (cover 398). What criminal could ever hope to outmuscle a man who juggles the
Eiffel Tower like a paperweight?

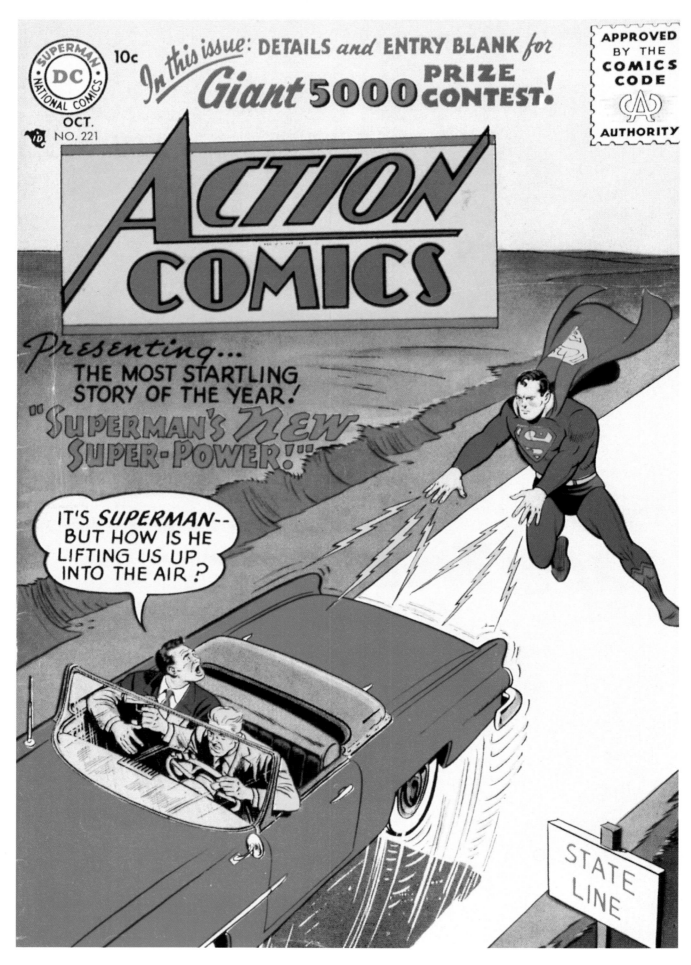

OCTOBER 1956; NO. 221
Cover artist: Al Plastino

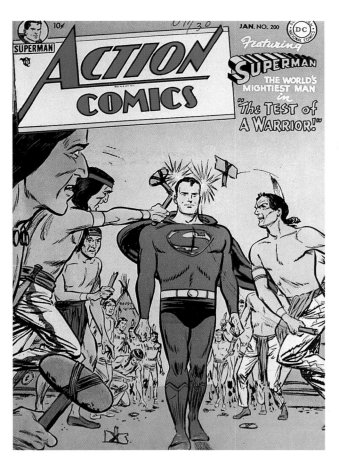

JANUARY 1955; NO. 200
Cover artist: Win Mortimer

FEBRUARY 1955; NO. 201
Cover artist: Al Plastino

JANUARY 1956; NO. 212
Cover artist: Al Plastino

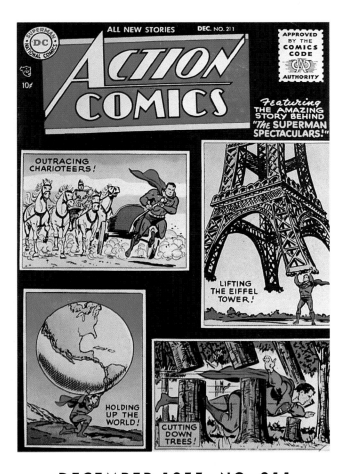

DECEMBER 1955; NO. 211
Cover artist: Win Mortimer

MARCH 1956; NO. 214
Cover artist: Al Plastino

SEPTEMBER 1958; NO. 244
Cover artists: Curt Swan, Stan Kaye

AUGUST 1957; NO. 231
Cover artists: Wayne Boring, Stan Kaye

MAY 1957; NO. 228
Cover artist: Al Plastino

MAY 1959; NO. 252
Cover artists: Curt Swan, Al Plastino

MAID OF MIGHT

Supergirl—a.k.a. Kara Zor-El, Superman's cousin—was the sole survivor of Argo City, a domed Kryptonian colony flung free of Krypton's explosion. Like her cousin before her, Kara was rocketed to Earth, where she gained the powers that made her a Girl of Steel.

As Superman's protégé, she began her career as his "secret weapon," but by the early 1960s, she'd come into her own not only as a heroine but as a full-fledged co-star. Supergirl's popularity with readers became so great that many covers showcased her adventures in lieu of Superman's. From March 1966 (cover 334) to April 1969 (cover 373), fans were treated to an additional issue of *Action Comics* each year, an annual giant-sized edition that re-presented some of the Maid of Might's greatest adventures.

MARCH 1966; NO. 334
Cover artists: Jim Mooney, Sheldon Moldoff

APRIL 1969; NO. 373
Cover artists: Curt Swan, Neal Adams

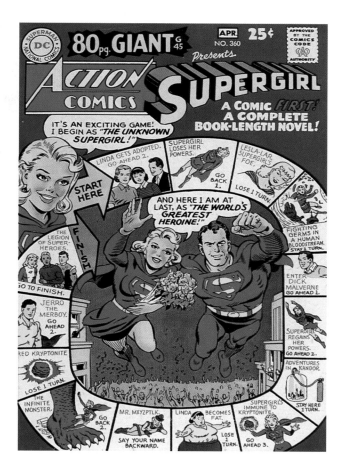

APRIL 1968; NO. 360
Cover artists: Curt Swan, George Klein

APRIL 1967; NO. 347
Cover artists: Curt Swan, George Klein

APRIL 1963; NO. 299
Cover artists: Curt Swan, George Klein

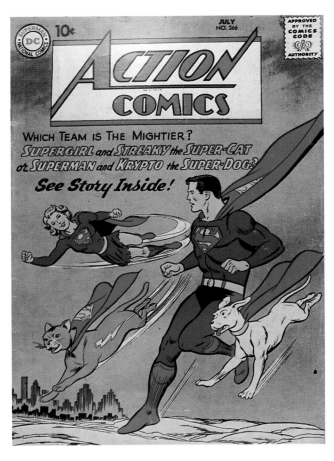

JULY 1960; NO. 266
Cover artists: Curt Swan, Stan Kaye

JUNE 1961; NO. 277
Cover artists: Curt Swan, Stan Kaye

20

JANUARY 1960; NO. 260
Cover artists: Curt Swan, Stan Kaye

OCTOBER 1962; NO. 293
Cover artists: Curt Swan, Sheldon Moldoff

APRIL 1966; NO. 336
Cover artists: Curt Swan, George Klein

JUNE 1962; NO. 289
Cover artists: Curt Swan, George Klein

SEPTEMBER 1964; NO. 316
Cover artists: Curt Swan, George Klein

MAY 1961; NO. 276
Cover artists: Curt Swan, Stan Kaye

FEBRUARY 1967; NO. 346
Cover artists: Curt Swan, George Klein

MAY 1965; NO. 324
Cover artists: Curt Swan, George Klein

JUNE 1960; NO. 265
Cover artists: Curt Swan, Stan Kaye

NOVEMBER 1959; NO. 258
Cover artists: Curt Swan, Stan Kaye

DECEMBER 1963; NO. 307
Cover artists: Curt Swan, George Klein

FEBRUARY 1962; NO. 285
Cover artists: Curt Swan, George Klein

JULY 1955; NO. 206
Cover artist: Win Mortimer

SUPERMAN'S SWEETHEART

Theirs was the first love triangle in history to involve only two people. Lois Lane, star reporter for the *Daily Planet*, ignored the amorous attentions of her rival Clark Kent; in her dreams, there was only one man who could take her to Cloud Nine. Ironically, that same man refused to win her hand unless he could do so as an ordinary mortal, insistent that Lois should prove she loved him for who he was, not what he could do. Though all secrets have since been revealed between the happy couple, the Lois Lane of the Silver Age was blissfully unaware that the man she loved and the milquetoast she loathed were in fact one and the same.

MARCH 1955; NO. 202
Cover artists: Wayne Boring, Stan Kaye

NOVEMBER 1960; NO. 270
Cover artists: Curt Swan, Stan Kaye

OCTOBER 1958; NO. 245
Cover artists: Curt Swan, Stan Kaye

DECEMBER 1959; NO. 259
Cover artists: Curt Swan, Stan Kaye

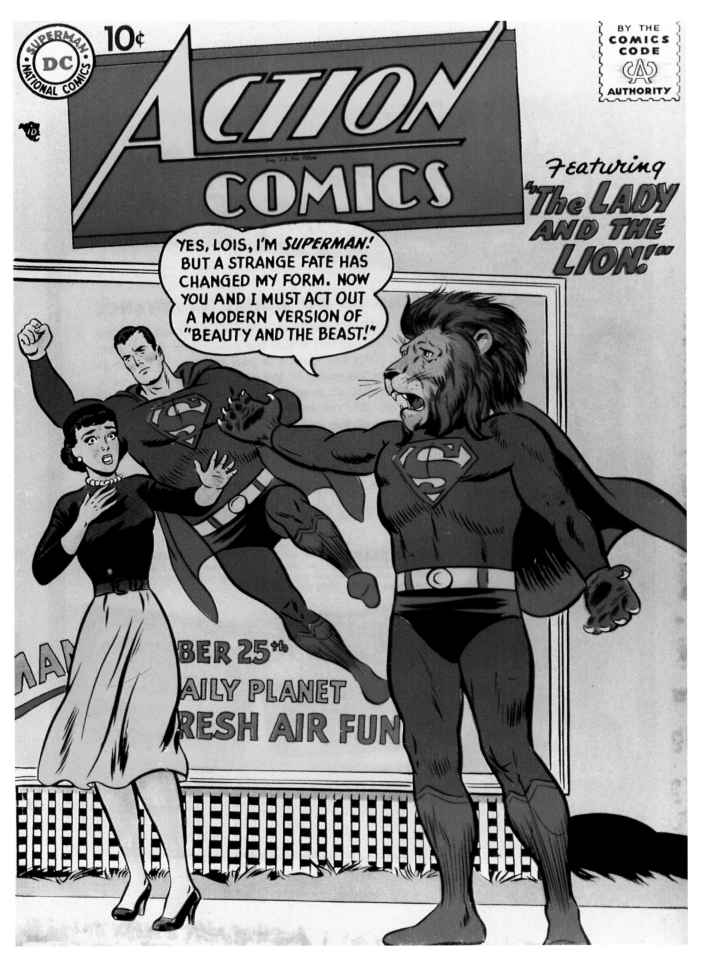

AUGUST 1958; NO. 243
Cover artists: Curt Swan, Stan Kaye

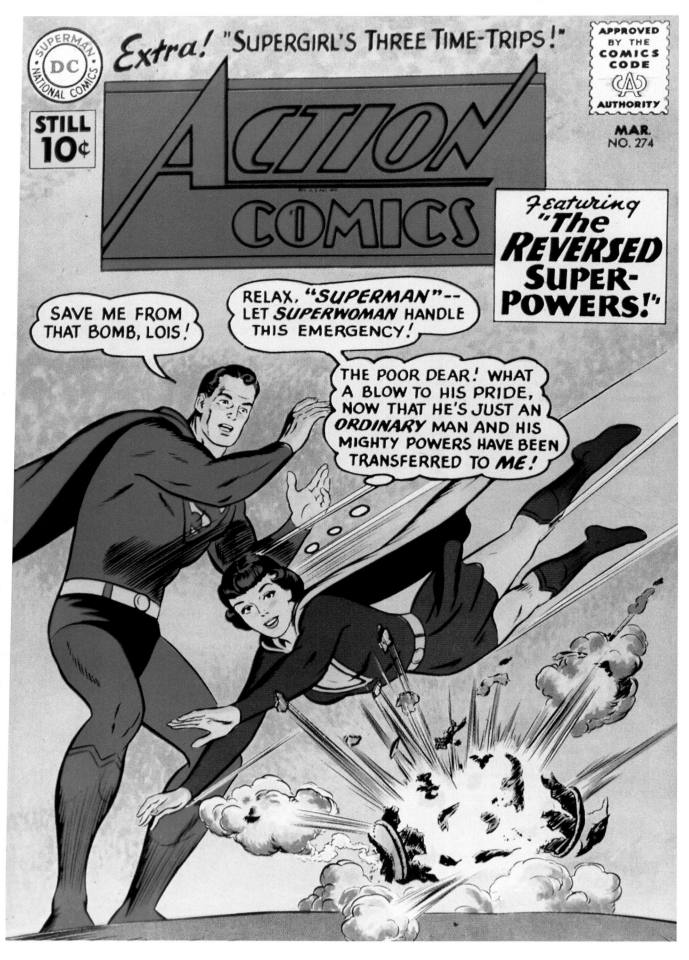

MARCH 1961; NO. 274
Cover artists: Curt Swan, Stan Kaye

JANUARY 1960; NO. 260
Cover artists: Curt Swan, Stan Kaye

AUGUST 1959; NO. 255
Cover artists: Curt Swan, Stan Kaye

SEPTEMBER 1960; NO. 268
Cover artists: Curt Swan, Stan Kaye

AUGUST 1961; NO. 279
Cover artists: Curt Swan, Stan Kaye

APRIL 1955; NO. 203
Cover artist: Al Plastino

MAY 1970; NO. 388
Cover artists: Curt Swan, Murphy Anderson

35

NOVEMBER 1957; NO. 234
Cover artists: Curt Swan, Stan Kaye

ENEMY OF EVIL

Evil wears many faces. It can attack in the form of a devil (cover 378) or a mischievous child (cover 315); it can even cloak itself in the guise of a trusted friend (covers 253, 278). But no matter what shape it takes, from Eterno (cover 343) to the Eliminator (cover 379), its menace can never overcome Superman's boundless courage.

Though each of Superman's battles is the stuff of legend, at least one was inspired by a real-world conflict: the circulation war between Superman and his once-fiercest newsstand competitor, Fawcett Comics' Captain Marvel, a caped champion who invoked the powers of the mythological gods by shouting the magic word "Shazam!" Though the good Captain was forced into retirement in 1953, depriving millions of young readers of the chance to see Superman and his rival duke it out for the championship title "World's Mightiest Mortal," *Action Comics* provided the next-best thing: a battle royal between the Action Ace and the thinly veiled "Zha-Vam" (covers 351, 353).

APRIL 1967; NO. 349
Cover artists: Curt Swan, George Klein

MARCH 1957; NO. 226
Cover artists: Wayne Boring, Stan Kaye

NOVEMBER 1966; NO. 343
Cover artists: Curt Swan, George Klein

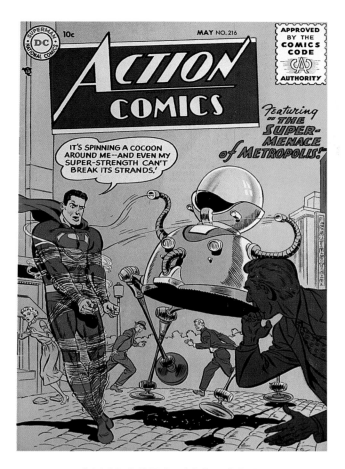

MAY 1956; NO. 216
Cover artists: Wayne Boring, Stan Kaye

DECEMBER 1960; NO. 271
Cover artists: Curt Swan, Stan Kaye

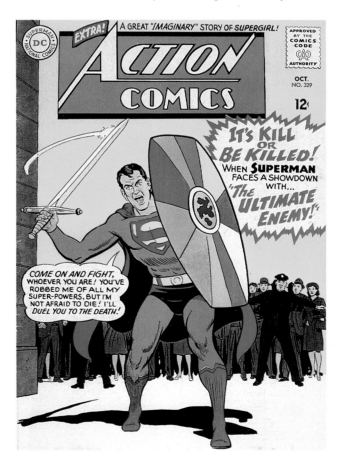

OCTOBER 1965; NO. 329
Cover artists: Curt Swan, Sheldon Moldoff

JULY 1965; NO. 326
Cover artists: Curt Swan, George Klein

JUNE 1959; NO. 253
Cover artists: Curt Swan, Stan Kaye

JULY 1961; NO. 278
Cover artists: Curt Swan, Stan Kaye

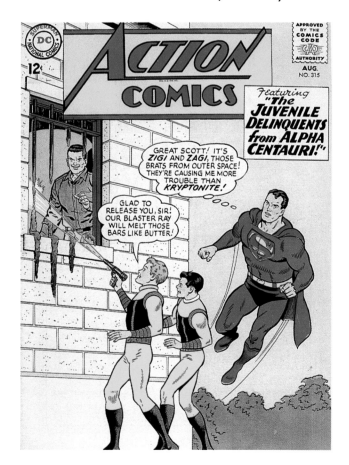

AUGUST 1964; NO. 315
Cover artists: Curt Swan, George Klein

OCTOBER 1955; NO. 209
Cover artists: Wayne Boring, Stan Kaye

AUGUST 1967; NO. 353
Cover artist: Wayne Boring

JUNE 1967; NO. 351
Cover artists: Curt Swan, George Klein

SEPTEMBER 1967; NO. 354
Cover artists: Curt Swan, George Klein

NOVEMBER 1967; NO. 356
Cover artist: Neal Adams

43

JULY 1969; NO. 378
Cover artists: Curt Swan, Neal Adams

NOVEMBER 1965; NO. 330
Cover artists: Curt Swan, George Klein

JANUARY 1961; NO. 272
Cover artists: Curt Swan, Stan Kaye

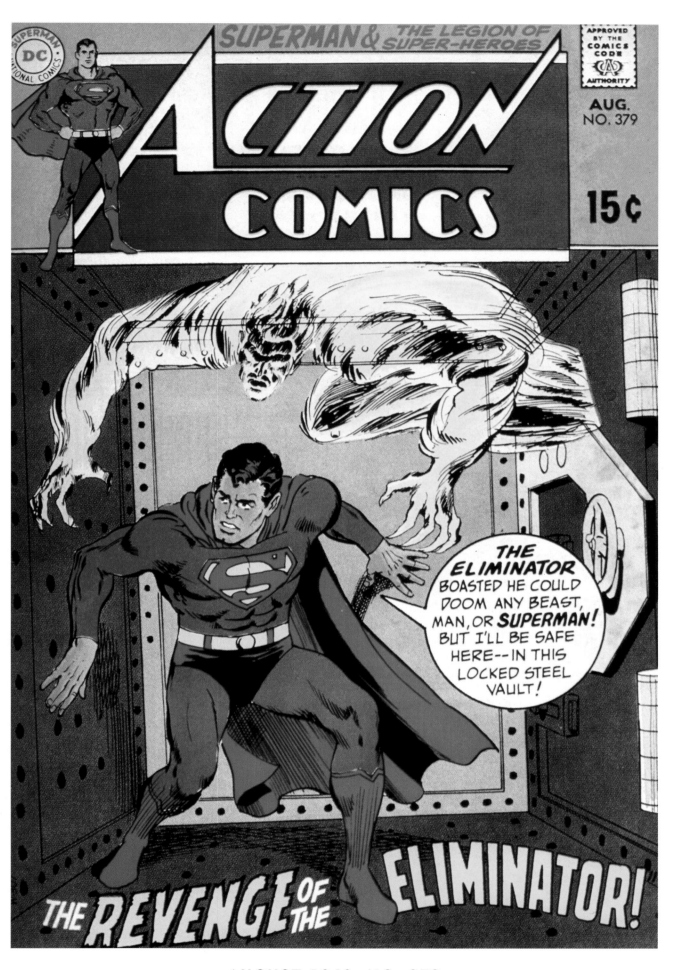

AUGUST 1969; NO. 379
Cover artists: Curt Swan, Neal Adams

SEPTEMBER 1955; NO. 208
Cover artist: Al Plastino

ARCHENEMIES

Superman can never afford to relax his guard. Each new adventure brings with it another nefarious foe, one bent on ensuring that the battle against evil remains never-ending. The Metropolis Marvel's most formidable villains include Lex Luthor, whose criminal brain is every bit as formidable as Superman's brawn; Brainiac, the super-computer android protected by a force field even Superman can't crack; Bizarro, an imperfect, warped duplicate of Superman who is every bit as mighty as the Man of Steel; the mischievous Mr. Mxyzptlk, sinister sorcerer from the Fifth Dimension; and the radiation-scarred Parasite, who can drain Superman's powers with a touch.

FEBRUARY 1959; NO. 249
Cover artists: Curt Swan, Stan Kaye

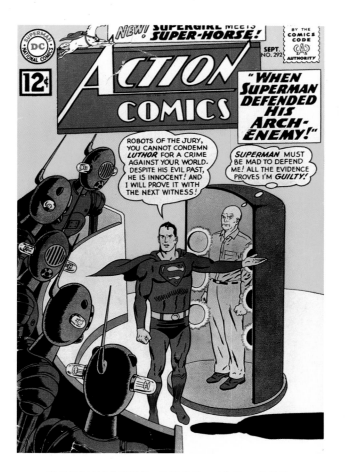

SEPTEMBER 1962; NO. 292
Cover artists: Curt Swan, George Klein

MARCH 1963; NO. 298
Cover artists: Curt Swan, Sheldon Moldoff

OCTOBER 1959; NO. 257
Cover artists: Curt Swan, Stan Kaye

DECEMBER 1959; NO. 259
Cover artists: Curt Swan, Stan Kaye

APRIL 1961; NO. 275
Cover artists: Curt Swan, Stan Kaye

JULY 1958; NO. 242
Cover artists: Curt Swan, Stan Kaye

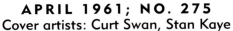

50

MARCH 1966; NO. 335
Cover artists: Curt Swan, Sheldon Moldoff

SEPTEMBER 1961; NO. 280
Cover artists: Curt Swan, Stan Kaye

FEBRUARY 1961; NO. 273
Cover artists: Curt Swan, Stan Kaye

JANUARY 1965; NO. 320
Cover artists: Curt Swan, George Klein

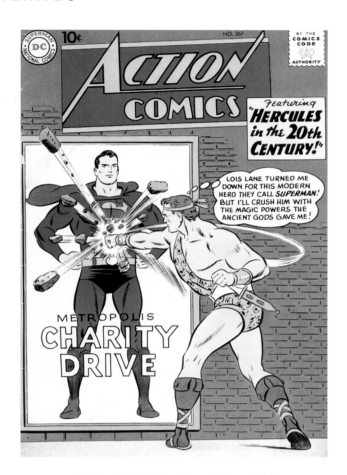

AUGUST 1960; NO. 267
Cover artists: Curt Swan, Stan Kaye

SEPTEMBER 1960; NO. 268
Cover artists: Curt Swan, Stan Kaye

AUGUST 1961; NO. 279
Cover artists: Curt Swan, Stan Kaye

JULY 1959; NO. 254
Cover artists: Curt Swan, Stan Kaye

AUGUST 1959; NO. 255
Cover artists: Curt Swan, Stan Kaye

APRIL 1960; NO. 263
Cover artists: Curt Swan, Stan Kaye

MARCH 1968; NO. 361
Cover artist: Neal Adams

AUGUST 1966; NO. 340
Cover artists: Curt Swan, George Klein

AUGUST 1962; NO. 291
Cover artists: Curt Swan, George Klein

KRYPTONITE

What color was kryptonite, that radioactive mineral poisonous to the Man of Steel? If you answered "green," you'd be only partly right, for during the Silver Age of *Action Comics* this otherworldly substance exhibited a dizzying rainbow of hues. Chief among them was the dreaded red kryptonite, a perennial favorite of writers otherwise stymied for ways to complicate Superman's life. Its effects were always completely unpredictable and, to Superman's regret, never beneficial; red kryptonite invariably put the Metropolis Marvel through any variety of freakish though temporary transformations. Blue kryptonite, though harmless to Superman, could kill Bizarro. And gold kryptonite was the most terrifying of all; even a moment's exposure to gold kryptonite would rob Superman of his powers forever!

MARCH 1964; NO. 310
Cover artists: Curt Swan, George Klein

MARCH 1960; NO. 262
Cover artists: Curt Swan, Stan Kaye

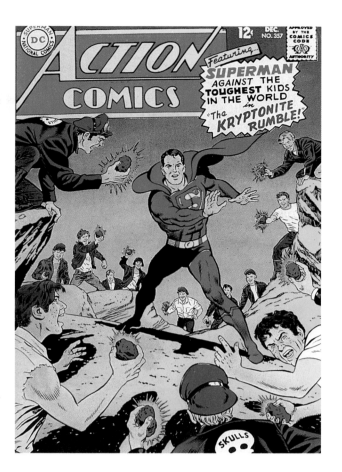

DECEMBER 1967; NO. 357
Cover artists: Curt Swan, George Klein

NOVEMBER 1963; NO. 306
Cover artists: Curt Swan, George Klein

JUNE 1969; NO. 377
Cover artists: Curt Swan, Neal Adams

DECEMBER 1961; NO. 283
Cover artists: Curt Swan, George Klein

JANUARY 1964; NO. 308
Cover artists: Curt Swan, George Klein

JULY 1962; NO. 290
Cover artists: Curt Swan, George Klein,
Kurt Schaffenberger

NOVEMBER 1962; NO. 294
Cover artists: Curt Swan, George Klein

OCTOBER 1966; NO. 342
Cover artists: Curt Swan, George Klein

OUT OF CONTROL

Superman is half policeman, half guardian angel to the people of Metropolis, and there is nothing he treasures more than their trust and faith in him. Through the years, he has jeopardized that trust only rarely, usually under the thrall of conniving criminals (cover 358) or synapse-scrambling amnesia (covers 372, 374). Outside influences have at times threatened to turn him into a super-assassin (cover 328) or a superhuman bomb (cover 342). Faced with even the direst circumstances, however, Superman invariably acquits himself of any true wrongdoing; nothing yet has managed to permanently tarnish the Man of Steel.

SEPTEMBER 1969; NO. 380
Cover artists: Curt Swan, Murphy Anderson

NOVEMBER 1968; NO. 369
Cover artists: Curt Swan, Mike Esposito

MARCH 1969; NO. 374
Cover artist: Neal Adams

JULY 1970; NO. 390
Cover artists: Curt Swan, Murphy Anderson

APRIL 1957; NO. 227
Cover artists: Wayne Boring, Stan Kaye

OCTOBER 1969; NO. 381
Cover artists: Curt Swan, Murphy Anderson

SEPTEMBER 1965; NO. 328
Cover artists: Curt Swan, George Klein

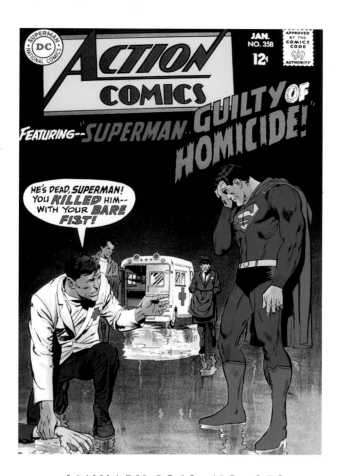

JANUARY 1968; NO. 358
Cover artist: Neal Adams

FEBRUARY 1969; NO. 372
Cover artists: Curt Swan, Neal Adams

SEPTEMBER 1968; NO. 367
Cover artists: Carmine Infantino, Neal Adams

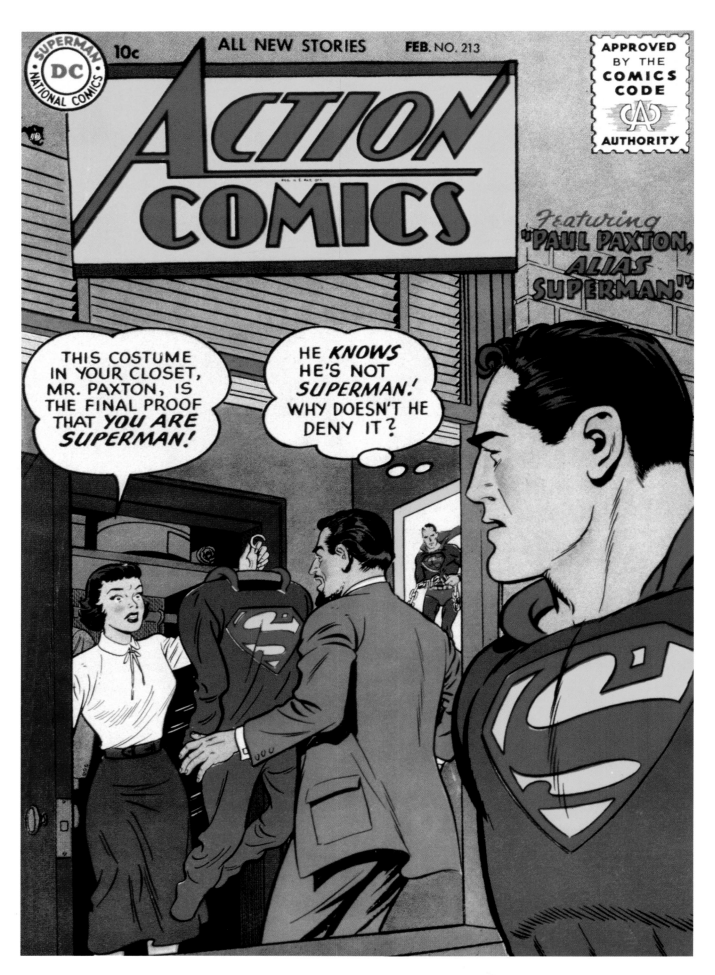

FEBRUARY 1956; NO. 213
Cover artist: Al Plastino

EXPOSÉ

A key element to Superman's lasting appeal has always been his alter ego—everyman Clark Kent. The fantasy that heroic power could be unleashed from behind a pair of glasses or from underneath ordinary street clothes was an idea that appealed mightily to bullied schoolkids everywhere.

The sanctity of the secret identity was of paramount importance to Superman; if criminals knew his dual identity, he reasoned, they would surely avenge themselves against Clark's friends and loved ones. Time and again, Superman has defended the secret from lie detectors (cover 250), magic mirrors (cover 269), television audiences (covers 288, 309, 345), and even his closest friends (covers 202, 282, 297, 313).

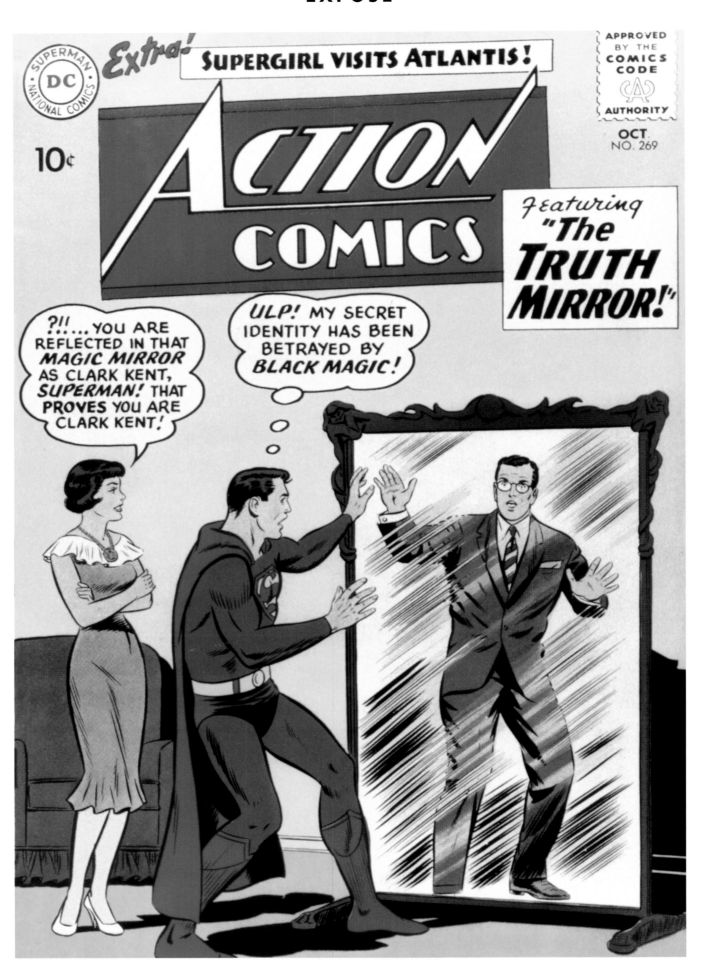

OCTOBER 1960; NO. 269
Cover artists: Curt Swan, Stan Kaye

JUNE 1964; NO. 313
Cover artists: Curt Swan, George Klein

JULY 1963; NO. 302
Cover artists: Curt Swan, John Forte

FEBRUARY 1963; NO. 297
Cover artists: Curt Swan, Unknown

FEBRUARY 1958; NO. 237
Cover artists: Curt Swan, Stan Kaye

MARCH 1955; NO. 202
Cover artists: Wayne Boring, Stan Kaye

DECEMBER 1965; NO. 331
Cover artists: Curt Swan, George Klein

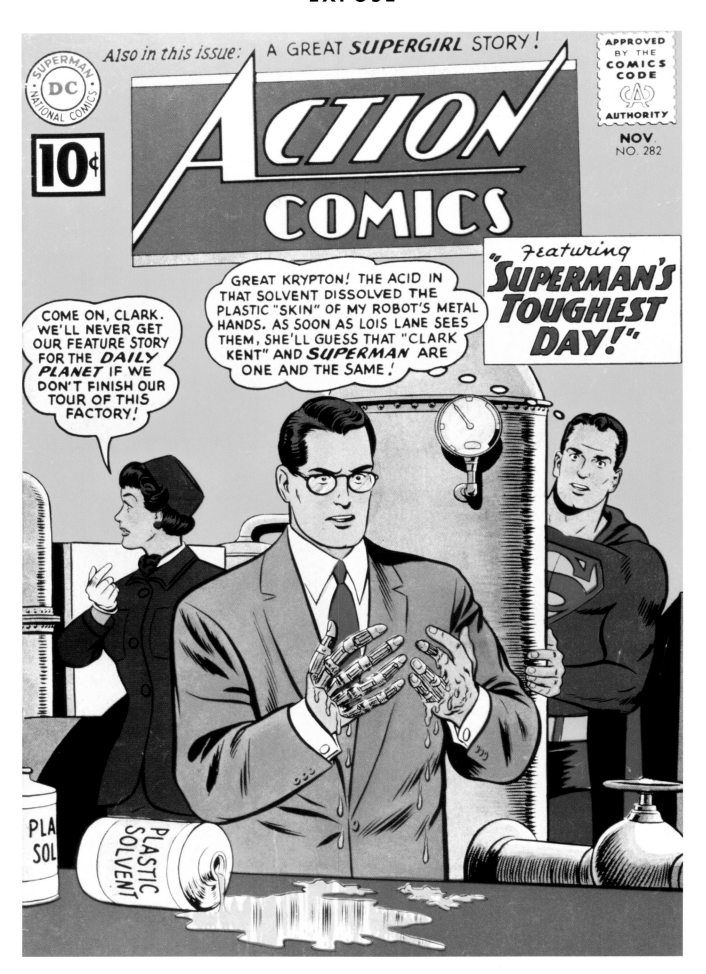

NOVEMBER 1961; NO. 282
Cover artists: Curt Swan, Stan Kaye

MAY 1962; NO. 288
Cover artists: Curt Swan, George Klein

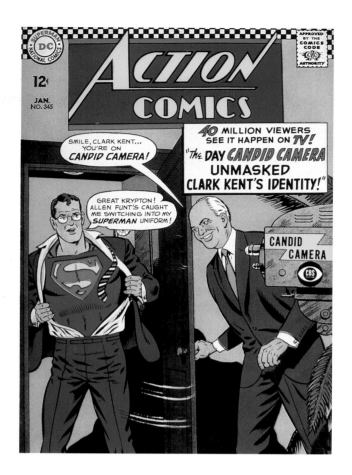

JANUARY 1967; NO. 345
Cover artists: Curt Swan, George Klein

FEBRUARY 1964; NO. 309
Cover artists: Curt Swan, Sheldon Moldoff

MARCH 1959; NO. 250
Cover artists: Curt Swan, Stan Kaye

OCTOBER 1963; NO. 305
Cover artists: Curt Swan, George Klein

APRIL 1968; NO. 362
Cover artist: Neal Adams

SEPTEMBER 1966; NO. 341
Cover artists: Curt Swan, George Klein

DUAL IDENTITY

As any prizefighter will tell you, a champion must always defend his title from those who would try to take it away— and the Krypton Kid has faced off against more than one caped poser. Though others have tried to mirror Superman (covers 222, 341), they have always proved themselves to be but pale reflections. From ancient times (cover 350) to future eras (cover 215), legions of pretenders have donned the familiar red "S" in hopes of replacing the Man of Steel . . . but in the end, they never seem to have the mettle. There's only one True Blue.

NOVEMBER 1956; NO. 222
Cover artist: Al Plastino

APRIL 1956; NO. 215
Cover artists: Wayne Boring, Stan Kaye

APRIL 1971; NO. 399
Cover artists: Neal Adams, Dick Giordano

OCTOBER 1957; NO. 233
Cover artists: Curt Swan, Stan Kaye

MAY 1967; NO. 350
Cover artists: Curt Swan, George Klein

AUGUST 1968; NO. 366
Cover artist: Neal Adams

JANUARY 1969; NO. 371
Cover artists: Curt Swan, Neal Adams

CLOTHES MAKE
THE
SUPERMAN

No one wears the same clothes every day—no matter how stylish and timeless the outfit—not even Superman. Occasionally, he experiments with different looks and even different roles. In his time, he's been a king (covers 311, 312), a president (cover 371), a soldier (cover 205), and a slugger (cover 389). He has exchanged his standard tights for suits familiar (cover 314), new (cover 236), and nefarious (cover 384). In fact, Clark Kent himself left his press pass behind once or twice in order to dabble in other occupations (covers 348, 382).

APRIL 1964; NO. 311
Cover artists: Curt Swan, Sheldon Moldoff

MAY 1964; NO. 312
Cover artists: Curt Swan, George Klein

JANUARY 1958; NO. 236
Cover artists: Curt Swan, Stan Kaye

JUNE 1955; NO. 205
Cover artist: Al Plastino

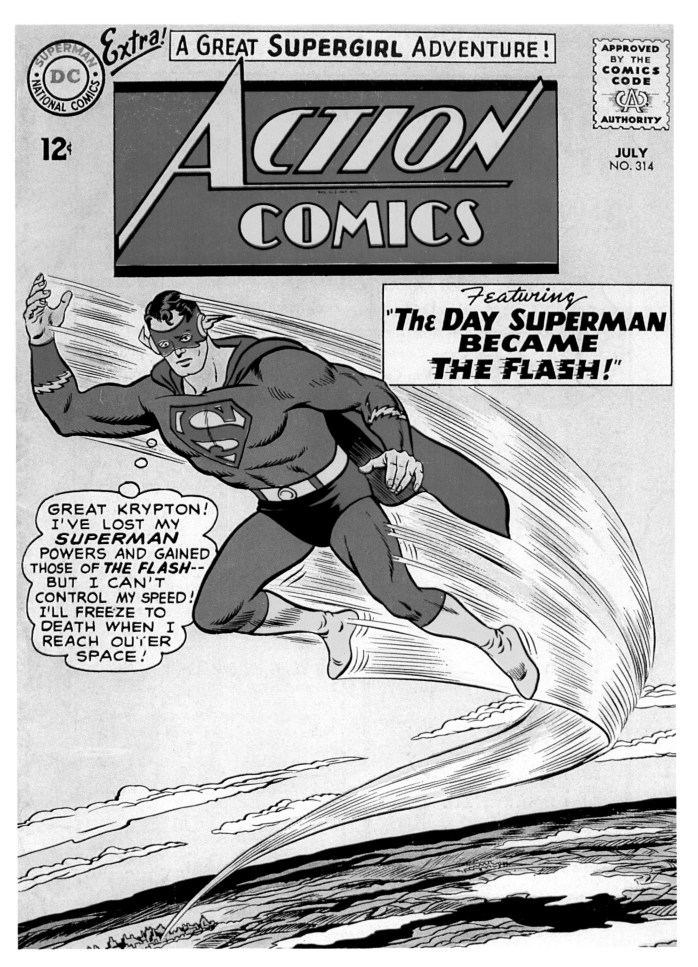

JULY 1964; NO. 314
Cover artists: Curt Swan, Sheldon Moldoff

JANUARY 1970; NO. 384
Cover artists: Curt Swan, Murphy Anderson

NOVEMBER 1969; NO. 382
Cover artists: Curt Swan, Murphy Anderson

MARCH 1967; NO. 348
Cover artists: Curt Swan, George Klein

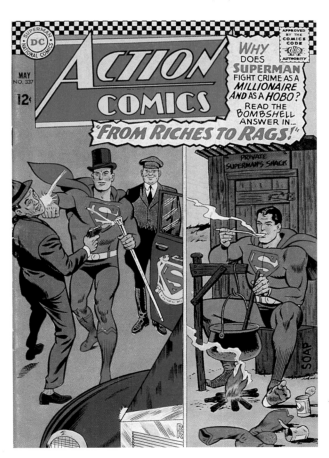

MAY 1966; NO. 337
Cover artists: Curt Swan, George Klein

JUNE 1970; NO. 389
Cover artists: Curt Swan, Murphy Anderson

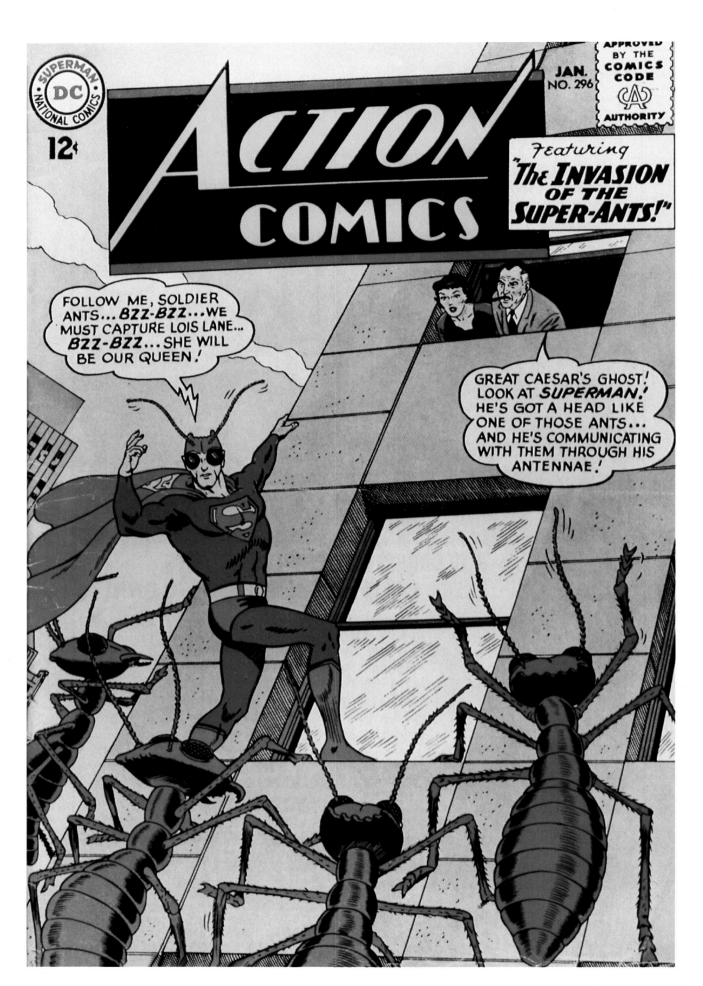

JANUARY 1963; NO. 296
Cover artists: Curt Swan, George Klein

STRANGE CHANGES

Weird forces often conspired to forge the Man of Steel anew. Magic spells and super-scientific devices alike twisted Superman through a number of transformations— from primal lion (cover 243) to future genius (cover 256), from young child (cover 284) to old man (covers 251, 270). Red kryptonite turned him into King of the Super-Ants (cover 296) and a horned Kryptonian dragon (cover 303), while the serpent-gaze of Medusa changed him into a Man of Stone (cover 352). Still, whether he was man or beast, underneath his familiar insignia beat the heart of a champion.

JULY 1967; NO. 352
Cover artists: Curt Swan, George Klein

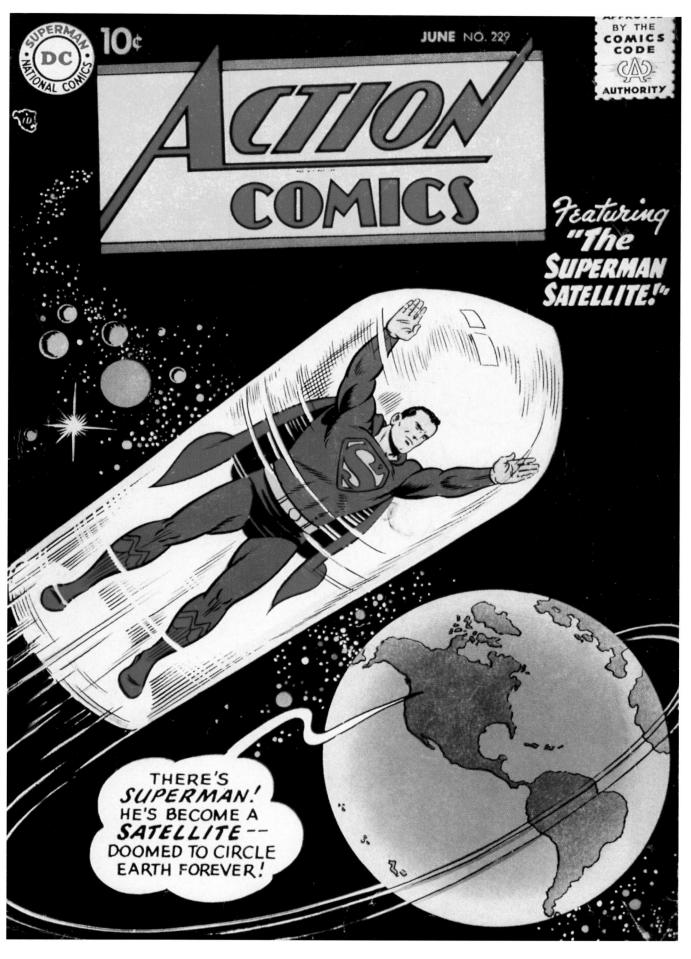

JUNE 1957; NO. 229
Cover artist: Al Plastino

NOVEMBER 1955 ; NO. 210
Cover artists: Wayne Boring, Stan Kaye

SEPTEMBER 1959; NO. 256
Cover artists: Curt Swan, Stan Kaye

MAY 1960; NO. 264
Cover artists: Curt Swan, Stan Kaye

OCTOBER 1964; NO. 317
Cover artists: Curt Swan, George Klein

JANUARY 1962; NO. 284
Cover artists: Curt Swan, Sheldon Moldoff

APRIL 1959; NO. 251
Cover artists: Curt Swan, Stan Kaye

NOVEMBER 1960; NO. 270
Cover artists: Curt Swan, Stan Kaye

AUGUST 1963; NO. 303
Cover artists: Curt Swan, George Klein

AUGUST 1958; NO. 243
Cover artists: Curt Swan, Stan Kaye

FEBRUARY 1966; NO. 333
Cover artists: Curt Swan, Sheldon Moldoff

JULY 1971; NO. 402
Cover artists: Neal Adams, Dick Giordano

DOWN AND OUT IN METROPOLIS

You can't keep a Superman down.

When the Action Ace made his debut in 1938, his powers were in a formative stage. He leapt, not flew; super-senses such as X-ray vision and super-hearing were a thing of the future; and while nothing less than a bursting shell could penetrate his skin, he had yet to face atomic bombs and laser beams.

By the 1960s, however, Superman was juggling planets, igniting suns with his heat vision, and flying through the time barrier unaided. Straining to incorporate suspense into the tales of an infallible god, editor Weisinger often compensated by stripping the Man of Steel of his powers for a month or two. Not only were readers better able to empathize with a powerless Superman, they learned by watching him persevere that the true hero is never the Super . . . but the Man.

SEPTEMBER 1963; NO. 304
Cover artists: Curt Swan, Sheldon Moldoff

FEBRUARY 1965; NO. 321
Cover artists: Curt Swan, George Klein

SEPTEMBER 1956; NO. 220
Cover artist: Al Plastino

MARCH 1965; NO. 322
Cover artists: Curt Swan, George Klein

JULY 1957; NO. 230
Cover artist: Al Plastino

MAY 1969; NO. 376
Cover artists: Curt Swan, Mike Esposito

APRIL 1962; NO. 287
Cover artists: Curt Swan, Sheldon Moldoff

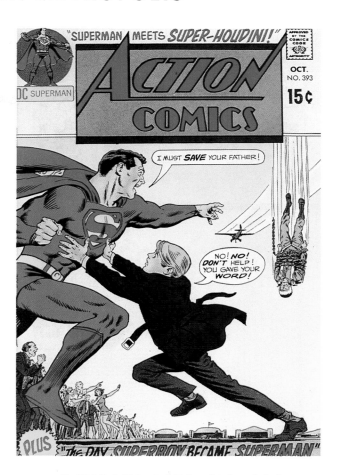

OCTOBER 1970; NO. 393
Cover artists: Curt Swan, Murphy Anderson

MARCH 1970; NO. 386
Cover artists: Curt Swan, Murphy Anderson

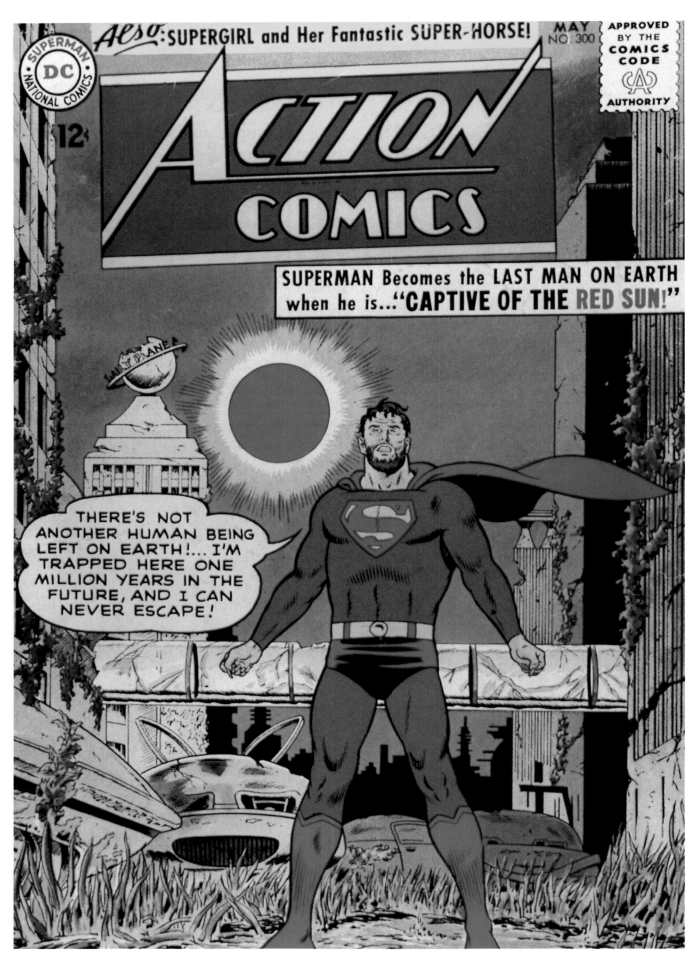

MAY 1963; NO. 300
Cover artists: Curt Swan, George Klein

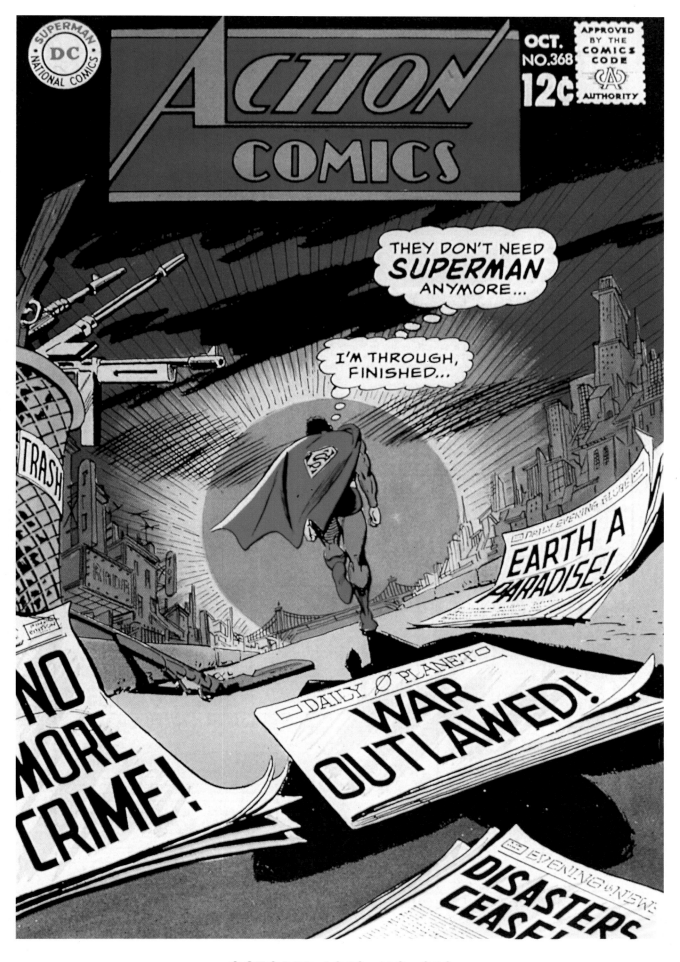

OCTOBER 1968; NO. 368
Cover artist: Carmine Infantino

FEBRUARY 1968; NO. 359
Cover artist: Neal Adams

FALSE ARREST

Given the thousands of crooks Superman has jailed during his long career, it's ironic that he himself has landed behind bars more than once, charged with acts of murder (covers 319, 359) and mayhem (cover 295). Since he has been known to bend steel in his bare hands, the shackle of choice is often a chain of kryptonite—though in a pinch, his own honor will hold him in custody until his name can be cleared or until justice prevails.

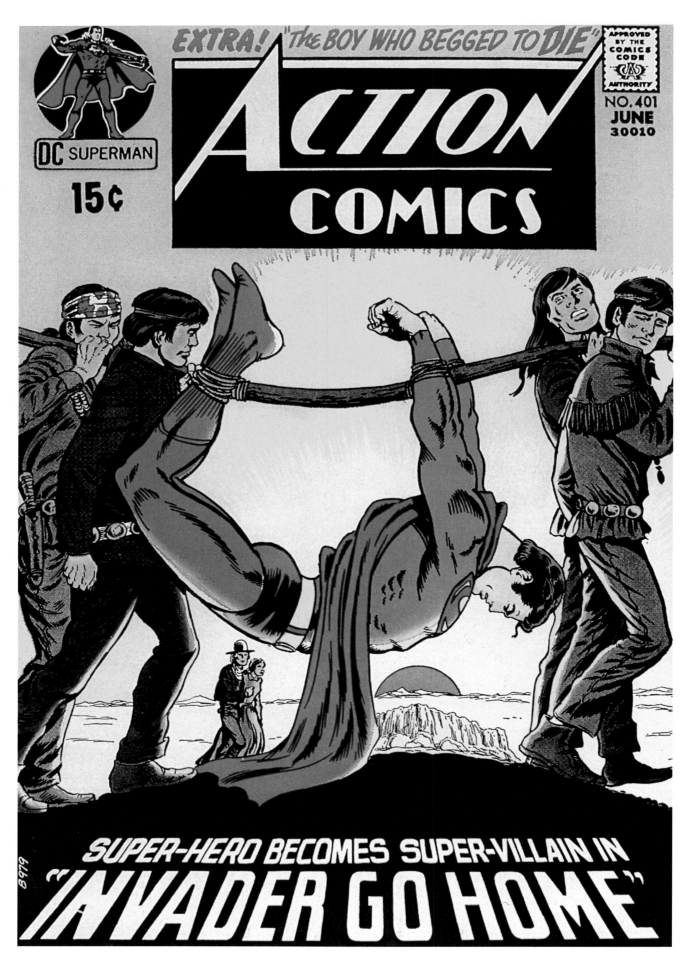

JUNE 1971; NO. 401
Cover artists: Neal Adams, Murphy Anderson

DECEMBER 1957; NO. 235
Cover artists: Curt Swan, Stan Kaye

DECEMBER 1962; NO. 295
Cover artists: Curt Swan, George Klein

NOVEMBER 1964; NO. 318
Cover artists: Curt Swan, George Klein

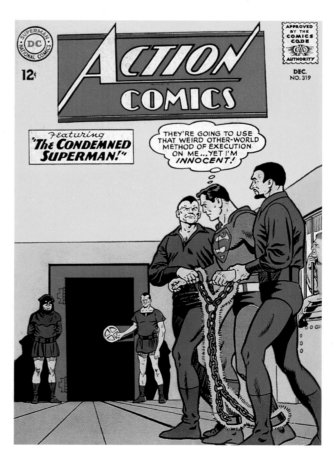

DECEMBER 1964; NO. 319
Cover artists: Curt Swan, George Klein

113

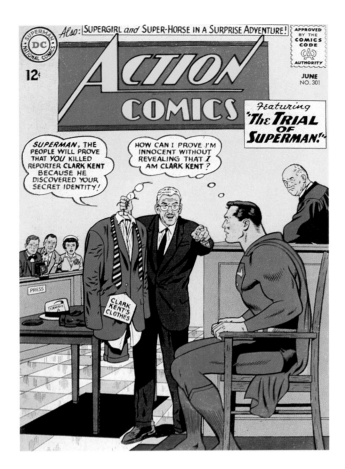

JUNE 1963; NO. 301
Cover artists: Curt Swan, George Klein

APRIL 1965; NO. 323
Cover artists: Curt Swan, George Klein

JANUARY 1959; NO. 248
Cover artists: Curt Swan, Stan Kaye

FEBRUARY 1970; NO. 385
Cover artists: Curt Swan, Murphy Anderson

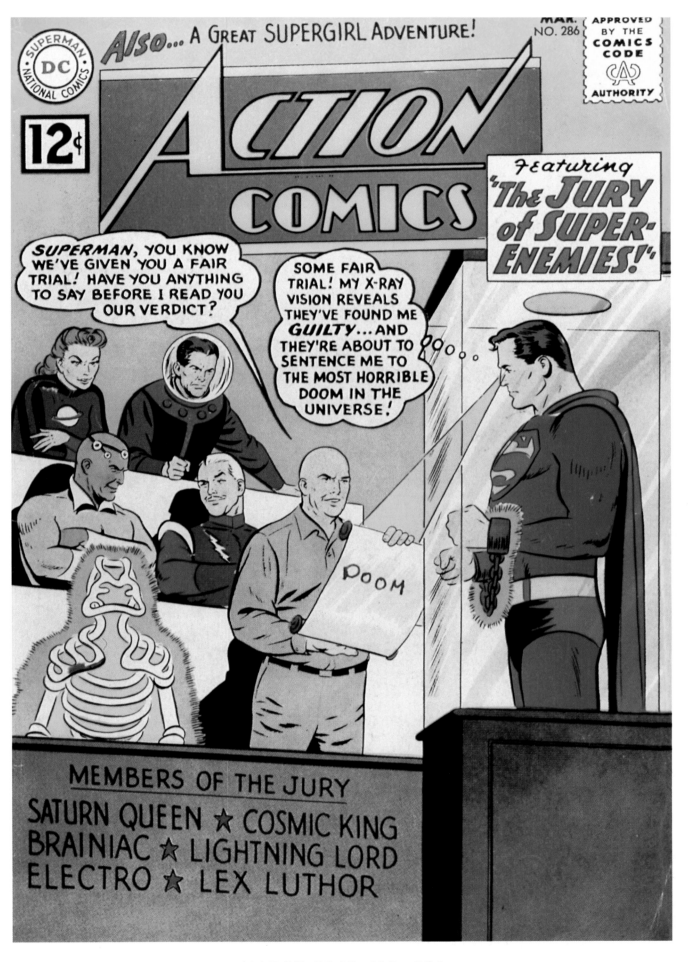

MARCH 1962; NO. 286
Cover artists: Curt Swan, Sheldon Moldoff

JULY 1968; NO. 365
Cover artists: Ross Andru, Mike Esposito

THE DEATH OF SUPERMAN

In 1992, real-world headlines told of Superman's untimely passing, but this wasn't the first time the Man of Tomorrow had dueled with the Grim Reaper. Though Superman had more than once faked his own death in order to roust criminals from their lairs, a landmark 1968 run of *Action Comics* (covers 363–65) told the tale of a Kryptonian leprosy known as Virus X—and how its ravages nearly claimed the Last Son of Krypton.

The cover of *Action Comics* 387 tells us that even a Superman dies. Chalk the claim up to editorial hyperbole. So long as there is a need for truth and justice, he will live forever.

APRIL 1970; NO. 387
Cover artists: Curt Swan, Murphy Anderson

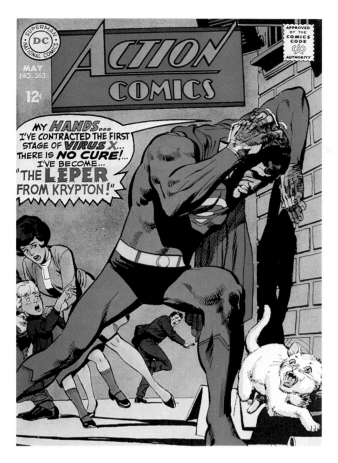

MAY 1968; NO. 363
Cover artist: Neal Adams

JUNE 1968; NO. 364
Cover artist: Neal Adams

FEBRUARY 1957; NO. 225
Cover artist: Al Plastino

AUGUST 1961; NO. 279
Cover artists: Curt Swan, Stan Kaye

JUST IMAGINE

Every Superman story begins the same way: the writer asks himself "What if . . . ?" What if Brainiac teamed with Luthor? What if Perry White somehow gained superpowers? Of course, there are some queries that can't be answered without permanently altering the Superman legend, such as "What if Krypton had never exploded?" or "What if Superman married Lois Lane?"

During the Silver Age of *Action Comics*, the editor nevertheless found a clever way to explore these questions through a series of "Imaginary Stories," what-if tales of adventure and intrigue that showed what Superman's life might be like if he had come to Earth after Supergirl (cover 332) . . . or if he were aged and retired (covers 396, 397) . . . or if he had children of his own (cover 327). In fact, several of these "Imaginary Tales" (covers 338, 339) didn't feature Superman at all—but rather the 30th-century descendant he might someday have.

JUNE 1966; NO. 338
Cover artists: Curt Swan, George Klein

JULY 1966; NO. 339
Cover artists: Curt Swan, George Klein

AUGUST 1965; NO. 327
Cover artists: Curt Swan, George Klein

JANUARY 1966; NO. 332
Cover artists: Curt Swan, Sheldon Moldoff

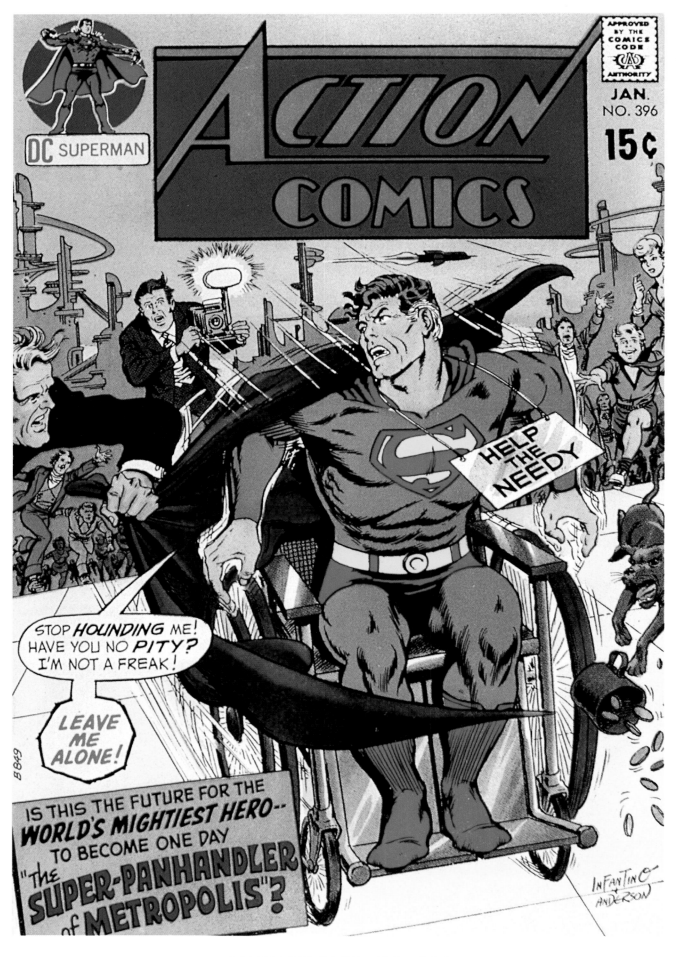

JANUARY 1971; NO. 396
Cover artists: Carmine Infantino, Murphy Anderson

FEBRUARY 1971; NO. 397
Cover artists: Carmine Infantino, Murphy Anderson

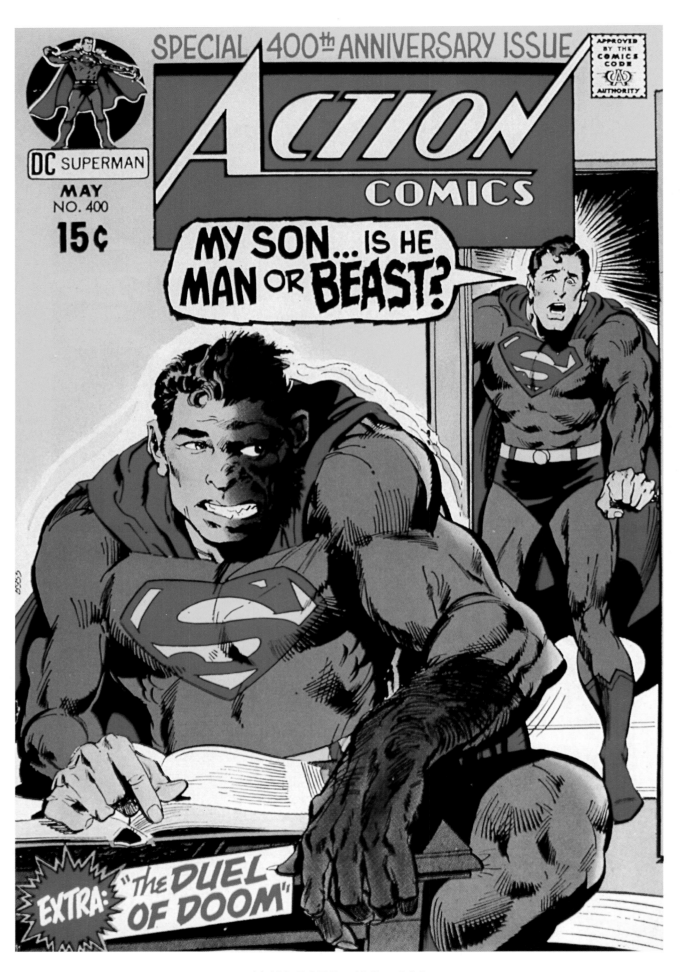

MAY 1971; NO. 400
Cover artists: Neal Adams, Dick Giordano

SUPER-SONS

Ironically, Metropolis's most eligible bachelor has often tasted the sweetness of family life. From time to time, children who have temporarily gained superpowers thanks to some freak spell (cover 400) or mystic meteor (cover 232) have offered to share his lonely crusade against evil. Most pull their weight; others, to the delight of a needling Batman, belly flop (cover 392). Once upon a time, Superman even became a super-son himself (cover 325), when an errant lab experiment turned the infant Kal-El into a giant tot who terrorized all Krypton!

SEPTEMBER 1957; NO. 232
Cover artists: Curt Swan, Stan Kaye

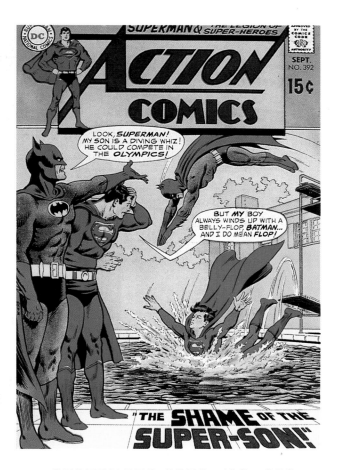

AUGUST 1970; NO. 391
Cover artists: Curt Swan, Murphy Anderson

SEPTEMBER 1970; NO. 392
Cover artists: Curt Swan, Murphy Anderson

JUNE 1956; NO. 217
Cover artist: Al Plastino

JUNE 1965; NO. 325
Cover artists: Curt Swan, George Klein

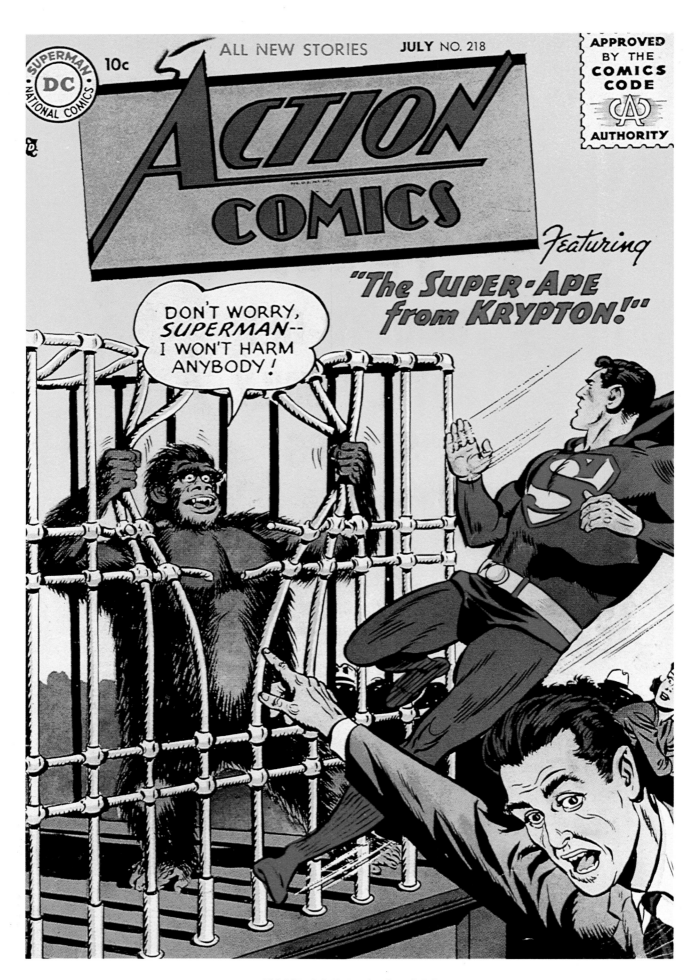

JULY 1956; NO. 218
Cover artists: Probably Wayne Boring, Stan Kaye

LAST SON OF KRYPTON

Throughout the Silver Age, *Action Comics* explored Superman's Kryptonian heritage, a vast and ever-growing tapestry woven with care and precision. No detail surrounding the doomed planet was too small or trivial; readers knew the citizenry's preferred mode of transportation (the Jor-El, a flying auto invented by Superman's father), how many days made up a Kryptonian year (438, each 27.79 Earth-hours long), and its most common metal (gold, spewed endlessly from a volcano on the north shore of the Bolenth continent). Attentive children of the 1960s probably knew more about Krypton than they did about their own hometown.

Superman seemed no less fascinated with Krypton than his readers—and small wonder. Lost artifacts and newfound survivors turned up with alarming regularity, always reminding Superman that, once, there was a place out in the great void of space that he called home.

OCTOBER 1961; NO. 281
Cover artists: Curt Swan, Sheldon Moldoff

NOVEMBER 1958; NO. 246
Cover artists: Curt Swan, Stan Kaye

DECEMBER 1968; NO. 370
Cover artist: Neal Adams

DECEMBER 1956; NO. 223
Cover artists: Wayne Boring, Stan Kaye

MARCH 1958; NO. 238
Cover artists: Curt Swan, Stan Kaye

JUNE 1958; NO. 241
Cover artists: Curt Swan, Stan Kaye

METROPOLIS MYSTERIES

The secret of Superman's dual identity wasn't the only mystery to tantalize Metropolis over the years. What eerie horror did their hero hide beneath mummylike bandages (cover 239)? Why would Superman, who could create diamonds from coal with the slightest squeeze of his superfist, hoard gold and greenbacks (covers 219, 394)? What truth lay behind his nightmare dreams (cover 344)? Does Superman pick the Killer Costume or the Ultra Uniform (cover 383)? How can he possibly overcome the ultimate identity crisis (cover 375)? And was there really—horror of horrors—a mere girl mightier than Superman (cover 395)? For a few precious cents, the answer was yours.

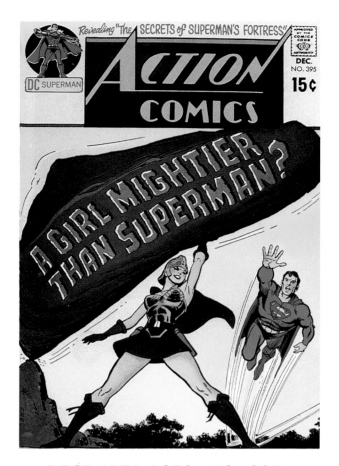

DECEMBER 1970; NO. 395
Cover artists: Curt Swan, Dick Giordano

DECEMBER 1958; NO. 247
Cover artists: Curt Swan, Stan Kaye

DECEMBER 1966; NO. 344
Cover artists: Curt Swan, George Klein

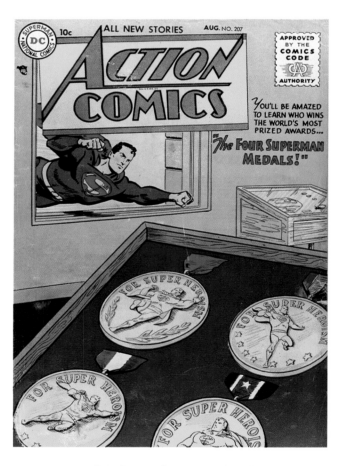

AUGUST 1955; NO. 207
Cover artist: Win Mortimer

FEBRUARY 1960; NO. 261
Cover artists: Curt Swan, Stan Kaye

NOVEMBER 1970; NO. 394
Cover artists: Curt Swan, Murphy Anderson

AUGUST 1956; NO. 219
Cover artists: Wayne Boring, Stan Kaye

MAY 1970; NO. 388
Cover artists: Curt Swan, Murphy Anderson

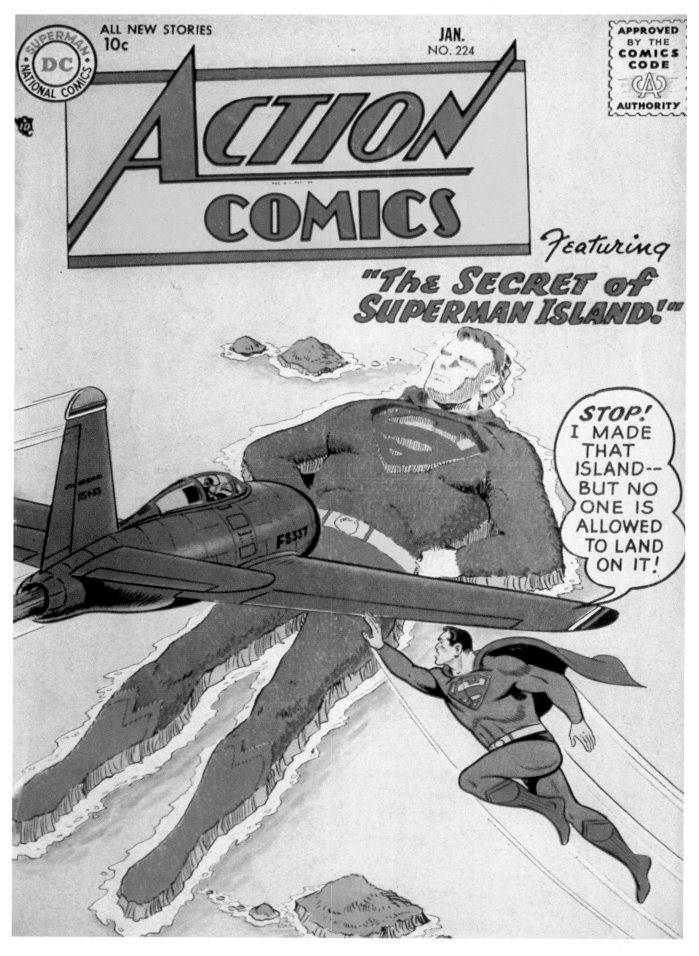

JANUARY 1957; NO. 224
Cover artist: Al Plastino

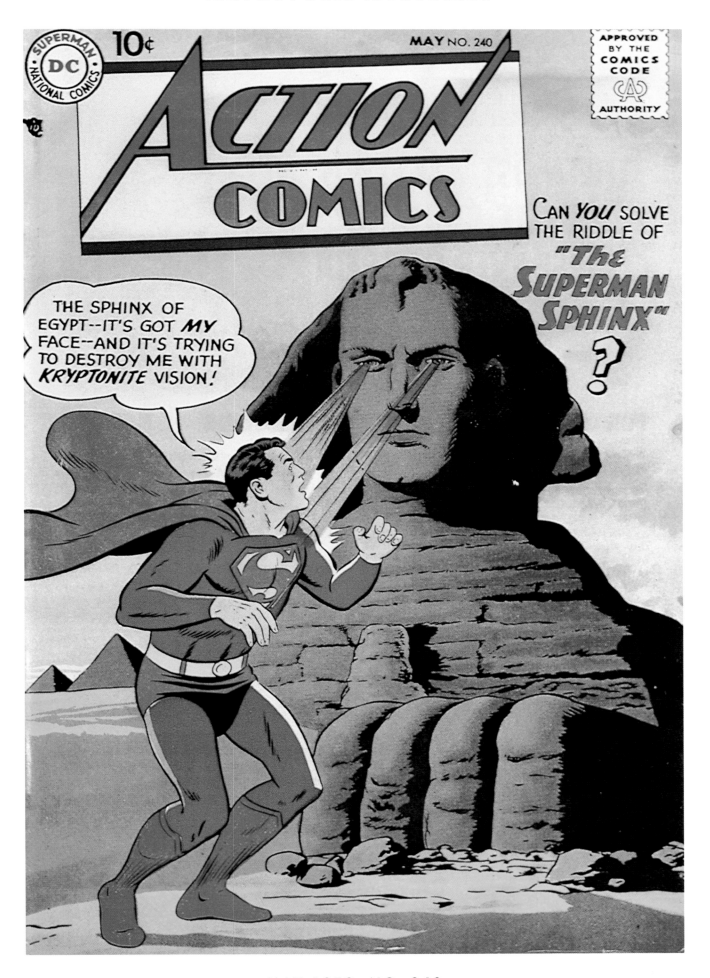

MAY 1958; NO. 240
Cover artists: Curt Swan, Stan Kaye

OCTOBER 1967; NO. 355
Cover artists: Curt Swan, George Klein

APRIL 1969; NO. 375
Cover artists: Curt Swan, Jack Abel

MAY 1955; NO. 204
Cover artist: Win Mortimer

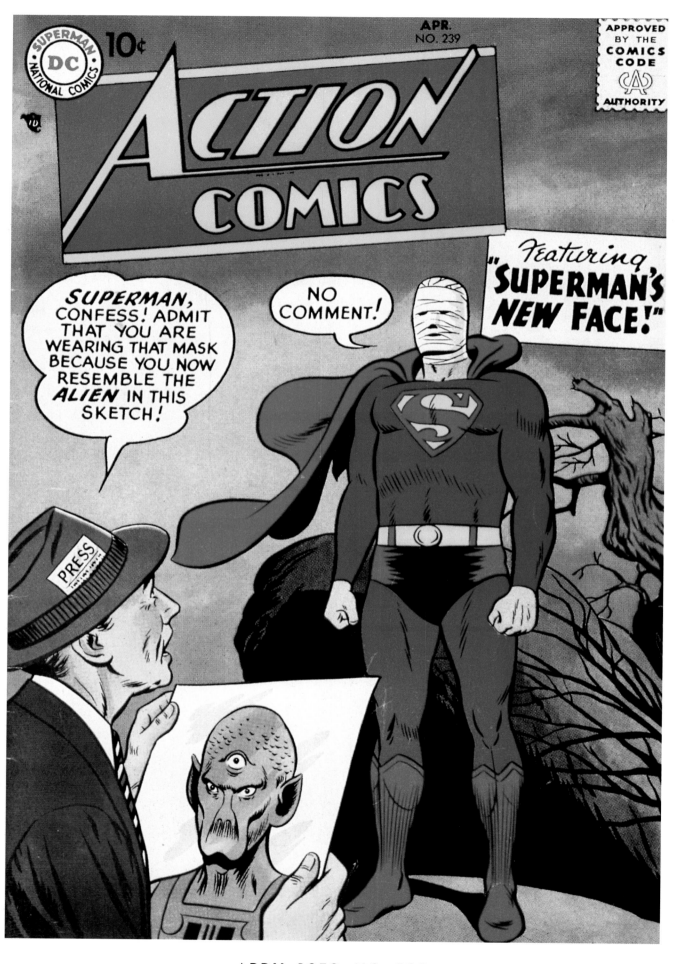

142

APRIL 1958; NO. 239
Cover artists: Curt Swan, Stan Kaye

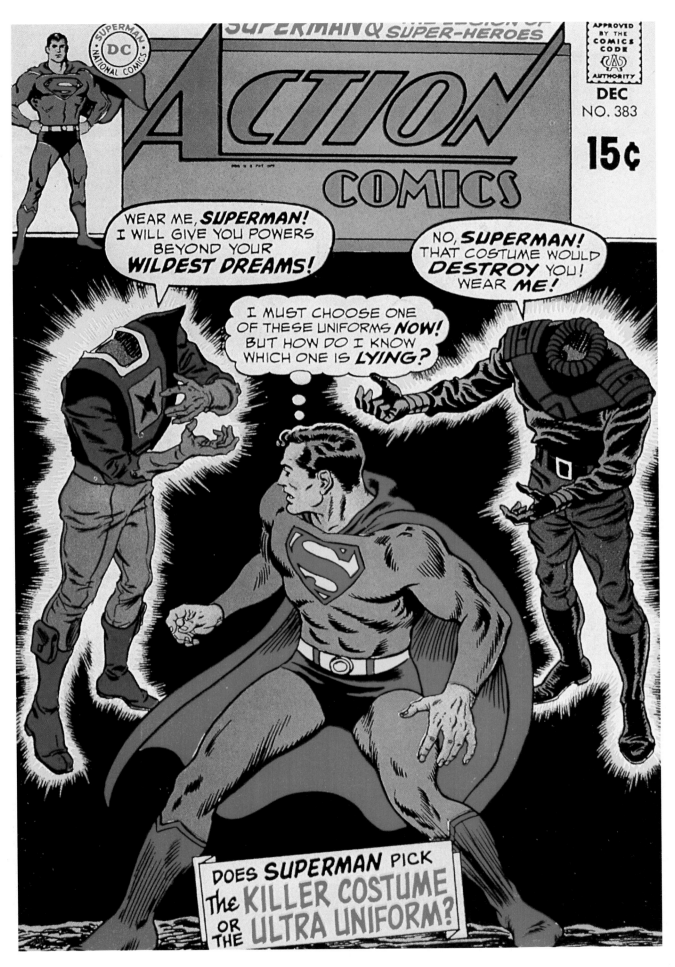

DECEMBER 1969; NO. 383
Cover artists: Curt Swan, Murphy Anderson

INDEX OF ARTISTS

Numerals refer to page—not issue—numbers.